Dogs and Puppies

Adria F. Klein

Dominie Press, Inc

Publisher: Christine Yuen
Series Editors: Adria F. Klein & Alan Trussell-Cullen
Editors: Bob Rowland & Paige Sanderson
Designers: Gary Hamada, Lois Stanfield, & Vincent Mao

Photo Credits: Graham Meadows (pages 4, 6, 8, 14, 16, 18-dogs);
Aaron Schall (pages 4, 8, 10, 12, 16, 18-girl).

Published by:

🔁 **Dominie Press, Inc.**

1949 Kellogg Avenue
Carlsbad, California 92008 USA

www.dominie.com

ISBN 0-7685-0563-1

Printed in Singapore by PH Productions Pte Ltd

2 3 4 5 6 PH 03

Table of Contents

I have a pet dog.
Her name is Happy.
She is a mother dog.
Happy is five years old.

I got her five years ago.
She was just a little puppy,
and I was just a little girl.
She has grown up with me.

Happy is going to
have puppies soon.
Her tummy has gotten
much bigger.
I can feel the baby puppies
moving around in her tummy.

One day I could not find Happy.
I looked for her everywhere.

I looked and looked for Happy,
but I could not find her.

That night, I went into my room.
Then I heard some noises.
The noises were coming
from my closet!
I got a flashlight,
and opened my closet door.

There was Happy.
And there were
four baby puppies!
The baby puppies
looked just like Happy.

The baby puppies grew and grew. Soon they were big enough to give away. I gave three of the puppies to three of my friends. I kept one puppy and named her Lucky.

One day I will be a big girl,
and Lucky will be a big dog.
Lucky will be as big as her mother.

I am so glad to have Happy
and Lucky. Maybe one day Lucky
will have baby puppies, too.

Picture Glossary

dog:

puppy:

flashlight:

Index